NEO-AUM SERMONS

ISAMU MICHI

NEO-AUM SERMONS

NEO-AUM SERMONS

Isamu Michi

ISBN-13: 978-0-9978363-5-6

ISBN-10: 0-9978363-5-0

martinetpress@protonmail.ch

FOREWORD

In March of 1995 the world at large became aware of Aum Supreme Truth when members of the group, including Ikuo Hayashi and Kenichi Hirose, carried out a deadly sarin attack in the crowded subways of Tokyo on a typically busy weekday underground at rush hour within the capital city of Japan. While the sarin failed to achieve the level of overarching lethality that the members of the group intended due to technical dispersion issues, the terrorist act brought to the forefront the lengths to which a hitherto little-known millenialist cult would go to bring about a doomsday scenario engendered by its founder Shoko Asahara and informed by a spiritual worldview and practice that had seemingly strayed very far indeed from that notable ksatriya who rejected caste society and sought enlightenment under a banyan tree in medieval Bihar so long ago.

In Satian 7 behind the idol of Nataraja - the form of Lord Siva who dances his dance of destruction at the world's end - lethal poisons flowed like the waters of dissolution through a complex system of chemical production and refinement apparatus built and watched over by engineers, physicists, accomplished organic chemists and a plethora of highly educated and highly capable persons coming from multiple interdisciplinary sciences. In a very real way the members of Aum Supreme Truth, acting as part and parcel of a collective under the direction of their enlightened master, were working in a palpable fashion to presence Lord Siva in his most destructive manifestation.

Much has happened for the erstwhile Aum communitarians in the intervening years since the sarin attack - the ban of the organization both domestically in Japan and within many other states, the incarceration of its principal leadership, including Shoko Asahara and the continuation of the group in different forms - existing under different names and operating under different fronts as tenacious and labyrinthine of the halls of its former headquarters in the shadow of Mount Fiji. What has and will remain a constant is the continual proliferation of the phenomena referred to by academics as New Religious Movements and the agency afforded via such groups to spiritual forces who seek a dynamic platform which many mainstream iterations of religion, calcified in their traditionalist posture, cannot or will not provide.

In Neo-Aum Sermons Isamu Michi, the author and founder of the Neo-Aum ideology, states in unequivocal terms that he has no compunction about inevitable (and seemingly invited, as his choice in nomenclature would indicate) comparisons between his group, worldview and ideology and that of the group who perpetrated the sarin attacks in the subways of Tokyo in a bid to preempt Armageddon. Neither does Michi claim any continuity with the original Aum Supreme Truth - nor association with groups who do possess such a continuity such as Aleph and the Circle of Rainbow Light, amongst others. Indeed, on a theological platform Michi's postulations are his own - emphasizing a broad if novel adherence to sectarian Vaisnavism rather than the titularly Buddhist model of Asahara's group. That said the devil, as ever, lies in the details.

As Aum Supreme Truth propitiated Lord Siva in his form of the inaugurator of the cataclysm prophecied to come at the end of the ages, Neo-Aum emphasizes devotion to Lord Visnu and Lord Kalki respectively. While the orientation of the latter is overt in its nature - the lila avatara who comes (literally) "not to bring peace, but with a sword" - also notable for the popularity of Lord Kalki among esoteric Hiterlists and all that might indicate - the emphasis on Visnu is not - or at least not at face value for the layman.

In the Srimad-Bhagavatam (and with Isamu Michi voicing a Srimad-Bhagavatam-centric cosmological worldview) Visnu is ever-present not as the preserver alone (the basis of the erroneous orientation which sends so many adherents of the Left-Hand Path running for the hills when confronted with this deity) but also as the destroyer of a nature even more over-arching in capacity and even more sinister in delivery than Lord Siva himself - though both work in tandem - with Visnu being the principal agent provocateur.

It is Visnu in the form of the thousand-headed serpent, Ananta Sesa, who telepathically communicates to Bhairava (a ghastly and dangerous form of Lord Siva) the means and methods of universal dissolution - wakening him from dormancy and stasis and it is Visnu who, in the form of the thousand-headed serpent rising up from the primordial waters of chaos who spews from his serpentine mouths the fire that burns the planets and aggregate material universes as Lord Kalki renders the earth to the state of an abattoir as he proceeds in his act of mass genocide.

Neo-Aum Sermons not only lionizes such apocalyptic concepts in sections such as Utopia Sermon and First, Second and Third Vision but transmogrifies them in a way distinctly characteristic of New Religious Movements and - furthermore - delineates in stark detail how adherents of Neo-Aum are perceived and expected to not simply be observers of but active participants in the bringing about of a new earth, the scope and properties of which are informed not only by traditional Vedic scripture but by the illumination of Neo-Aum practitioners themselves and the revelations of its credentes.

In this, Neo-Aum exists and presents itself as a fifth column against a failing and fallible humanity on behalf of its deity and transcendental creed with a hand extended for those willing to extricate themselves from the mire of a materialism gone mad and embrace an alternative through stringent practice of fervent devotion and active devotional service, with all that that might entail.

With that devotional service in mind and to the glories of the Supreme Personality of Godhead to which Neo-Aum adheres, Martinet Press first and foremost presents this published volume of Isamu Michi's work to the loyalists of Neo-Aum itself - the monks and nuns of its order and the workers past, present and future - as well as devotees still incipient.

Secondly we present this to the students of New Religious Movements whether they be in academe or engaging in independent study, with the axiom that those who do not remember the past are doomed to repeat it inclusive and in mind and thirdly to the broader readership itself, last but not least, in hope that Neo-Aum Sermons may provide a platform toward a vision of an alternate worldview. Worthy of contemplation and, for some, a prompt toward practice - however stringent - for the most celestial of fruits, ripe for the tasting, are often cultivated in the hardest of soils.

- Martinet Press

SERMON 1: MATERIALISM

I see so much materialism in this world which serves to give people only small amounts of pleasure. Instead of materialism which only brings small pleasure, people should focus on spiritual pleasure, which can be found through practice of Meditation and Yoga as well as pure fanatical love and devotion to Sri Vishnu. When the final avatar of Sri Vishnu appears, he shall not have come to convert people, he will have come to cleanse the earth of the unenlightened people. So I say to you now, spread the message, study the Vedas and Gita, find enlightenment through pure Yoga, Meditation and love and devotion to Sri Vishnu, and I do not mean simple harmless love between a man and woman. I mean Fanatical Love, for it is only through this Fanaticism to Sri Vishnu shall guide us upon the path to Enlightenment, the path of Truth.

SERMON 2: DEVOTION

I have taken some time to Meditate, and I have realized a fundamental flaw which is rarely Addressed among servants of Sri Vishnu. The flaw is that most Devotees are too relaxed in their service to the Supreme Personality of GodHead. There must be Cultic Devotion to Sri Vishnu if one truly desires to attain enlightenment through the Truth which only Sri Vishnu can show the way.

SERMON 3: AUM AND NEO-AUM

Aum Supreme Truth was an Organization formed and operated by Master Shoko Asahara, and it is from Aum Supreme Truth that I began forming my philosophy as well as laying the foundation for Neo-Aum. There will be bad press regarding the relation between Aum and Neo-Aum, and that is expected. It matters not what those on the outside think, it matters only what those on the inside think. Aum was definitely a clear example of what most people picture as a Cult. Neo-Aum is very much a Cult as well, in that I require absolute devotion by those who join Neo-Aum, because absolute devotion is needed to advance on the path of Truth.

SERMON 4: HONOR

Members of Neo-Aum must act honorably, so to avoid bringing Bad Karma on oneself. Anyone who does not act honorably shall be punished, and in the worst case, shall be expelled from Neo-Aum.

SERMON 5: THE LAW OF NEO-AUM

The Law of Neo-Aum is simple, all Members must be with Honor in all that they do, and the only Law that Members obey is The Law of Neo-Aum. Those who fail to understand and obey The Law of Neo-Aum shall be subject to discipline.

SERMON 6: PAIN

Pain is used within Neo-Aum to train and harden its Members as well as ensure that Members of Neo-Aum obey The Law of Neo-Aum and behave with Honor. Neo-Aum uses punishment to correct disobedience so that Members can take their experiences and training to progress on the Path of Truth. The Methods of Pain are kept secret, and are only taught to Members of Neo-Aum.

SERMON 7: MONKS AND NUNS

Members of Neo-Aum are the trusted Monks and Nuns who must take the message of Neo-Aum and spread it to all people, in all walks of life. Those who do this shall bring themselves good Karma, while those who fail to do this shall only bring themselves bad Karma. Bringing oneself good Karma pleases Sri Vishnu which is good. Bringing oneself bad Karma displeases Sri Vishnu which is bad.

SERMON 8: FORSAKE THE WORLD

I encourage Members of Neo-Aum to Forsake the World, what this means is to leave behind all that distracts one from worship of Sri Vishnu and the path of Truth. I encourage this because the World has too many distractions and if one cannot ignore these distractions they can bring bad Karma which can cause Members to stumble off the path to Enlightenment.

SERMON 9: MEDITATION

Members of Neo-Aum must Meditate daily, the Meditation requires focusing upon the symbol of Neo-Aum while thinking of Sri Vishnu. Members must also chant the Hare Krishna Mantra during meditation. Chanting The Hare Krishna Mantra during Meditation shall bring Members of Neo-Aum closer to Sri Vishnu as well as aid in developing the Fanatical love one needs to become a Perfect Devotee of Sri Vishnu.

SERMON 10: SPIRITUAL WORK AND MATERIALISTIC WORK

Members of Neo-Aum are expected to perform Spiritual Work, which is Worship of Sri Vishnu, Study of the Vedas and Gita, and spreading the message of Neo-Aum. Members are not allowed to peform Materialistic Work, which is all things which are not beneficial for Sri Vishnu or Neo-Aum.

For further information please contact me by Email: isamumichi3@gmail.com

Show support and join on Facebook page: NEO-AUM

Follow me on Facebook: Isamu Michi

THE EVILS OF INDIVIDUALISM

"One's True Self, though it is hard to describe, means what constitutes the root of oneself."- Master Shoko Asahara

The Roots of oneself is Sri Vishnu, who is the Root of all things, though most people shall deny this fact and they will continue to hold on to the illusion of Individual thoughts and ideas. To hold on to Individual thoughts and ideas is to hold back oneself from attaining Enlightenment. So it is the Mission of Neo-Aum to cleanse the minds and bodies of our members so that they will become void of any and all Individuality. This is so that they can progress forward toward the Truth. This is not an easy process however because Members must give up their illusions which they have been taught are real since their birth into this World. So I say now to all who are reading this, You must Join Neo-Aum and accept Sri Vishnu, that is Your only way to reach True Enlightenment in this world. Enlightenment is Mankind's only way to leave behind the cycle of Suffering which is caused by the Illusion of Existence.

THE ILLUSION OF LOVE BETWEEN HUMANS

The Illusion of Love is the most destructive and painful Illusion present on this planet, and it is one that cannot be escaped without Devotion to Sri Vishnu. I have Loved and Lost, and it is that Loss which causes the most pain and suffering. So I say to You now to redirect that Love to Sri Vishnu, for it is Sri Vishnu who shall never leave You, no matter what the situation may be. As long as You Love Sri Vishnu with absolute Fanaticism, Sri Vishnu shall always Love You back.

ALIENS AND THE PATH OF TRUTH

For many ages Extraterrestrial beings have visited this planet, and aided in the evolution of Humanity Through bestowing upon a few The Supreme Truth. These beings have also been worshipped as Gods due to the knowledge that they can bestow, which is precisely why Religion exists, but make no mistake. These Alien Gods have every right to be worshipped by a primitive race like Humanity, because to Humans they truly are Gods.

SUNFLOWER SERMON

The Monks and Nuns of Neo-Aum are as a field of Sunflowers, which if tended to properly shall bring Good Karma and Good Results. However if they are not tended to properly they shall dry and decay and become useless, which shall bring only Bad Karma and Bad Results. Those that dry up and decay shall be swiftly pulled out by the roots as to protect the rest of the field, however those that prosper and grow shall be carefully aided and tended to, as to bring a good harvest to be offered to Sri Vishnu.

NEO-AUM COMMUNE SERMON

The Monks and Nuns of Neo-Aum should strive to create a Commune, in which Sri Vishnu is the Supreme Authority and Master. Within a Neo-Aum Commune the only Law will be that of Sri Vishnu, this is very different from the Laws of the so-called "Modern Society" which we are enslaved by in this day and age. In a Neo-Aum Commune the Monks and Nuns shall Live an entirely Spiritual Life, which is free of any and all distractions from their Spiritual Growth which can only be found through Complete devotion to Sri Vishnu. Neo-Aum Communes are absolutely needed in all places to prepare people for the arrival of Sri Kalki who shall Cleanse and Purify this World of all who are not Enlightened by The Supreme Truth.

PSYCHOLOGY SERMON

Psychology is only for Unenlightened Humans, it is that simple. This is because instead of focusing upon Spiritual Health, Psychology focuses upon the Health of the Mind, which is nothing more than one of the many Illusions on this planet. Psychology can never truly provide a cure for "Illnesses" of the Mind, because they are just that, in the Mind. If a person is ever to truly get past their issues, they must focus upon Spiritual Health instead of Mental Health. The solution for Psychology is to drug up all those who have so called "Mental Problems", the solution for Neo-Aum is to teach people to avoid trusting Psychologists and to instead rely upon Sri Vishnu, who shall provide a real cure for the sufferer, instead of a fake cure which is given by Psychologists.

HONOR AND DISHONOR SERMON

Honor and Dishonor are very important when relating to Neo-Aum, this is because if a Monk or Nun acts with Honor then Sri Vishnu shall look upon Neo-Aum with only Positive Eyes and shall bestow only Good Karma upon all Monks and Nuns involved. If a Monk or Nun acts with Dishonor, then Sri Vishnu shall look upon Neo-Aum with only Negative Eyes and shall bestow only Bad Karma upon all Monks and Nuns involved.

SEX SERMON

Sex must be carefully Monitored by Neo-Aum, this is because too much Sex can distract from Spiritual Advancement, and lead to Bad Karma. Monks and Nuns are Forbidden to have Sex unless it is directly Approved by Neo-Aum. Having Sex with the Approval of Neo-Aum shall bring the Monks and Nuns participating only Good Karma. However, having Sex without the Approval of Neo-Aum shall bring only Bad Karma to the Monks and Nuns who are participating.

SUFFERING SERMON

Suffering, just as love is, are both only Illusions, though they are both Powerful, they are still simply Illusions, which can be overcome if You choose to Devote Your life to Sri Vishnu, who is capable of removing Negativity and Bad Karma from Your life, and replacing it with Positivity and Good Karma. The only way this can occur however is by Studying the Gita, and the Vedas and Joining Neo-Aum to further Your Spiritual Journey to attain The Supreme Truth, which is only attainable through Fanatical Devotion to Sri Vishnu.

FAMILY SERMON

In the Gita, it is warned to not become attached to Materialistic things such as Family, this is because Family only brings more Illusions into the lives of Monks and Nuns. It is for this reason that I encourage all Monks and Nuns leave behind their Family, and to accept that only the Spiritual Family of Neo-Aum is Important. The Spiritual Family of Neo-Aum offers the way to Truth, while the Materialistic Family offers only the way to Illusion.

LAMENTING SERMON

The Gita says that the wise Lament for neither the living or the dead, and this is a very true teaching. Such Lamentation shall only bring Illusions such as Sadness and Suffering into the life of a Monk or Nun, which shall hinder their Spiritual Progress. In times of Lamentation it is best to acknowledge Lamentation as only one of the many passing Illusions present upon this world, which too shall vanish through Devotion to Sri Vishnu.

IMPERMANENCE SERMON

The Monks and Nuns of Neo-Aum must understand Impermanence in order to advance further on The Path of Truth. Impermanence means nothing is forever, meaning the Illusions of this world will pass on as shall all of Us. However, unlike the Illusions of this world, We shall not simply cease to exist, but shall instead be taken to a Higher State of existence through Sri Vishnu who shall teach us The Supreme Truth, which all Monks and Nuns of Neo-Aum understand is the only way to reach True Enlightenment.

DEATH AND SUICIDE SERMON

Death must be understood by the Monks and Nuns of Neo-Aum, as the Key to freeing the Soul from the Flesh, which only serves as a prison to an Enlightened Monk or Nun. I am not stating this as an excuse for pointless Suicide, but I am giving this teaching as a reminder that Death by one's own Hand is a Sin, unless it is done in Complete Fanatical Devotion to Sri Vishnu. Those Monks or Nuns who choose to escape their Flesh prison, may choose any method of Suicide, as long as they recite the Hare Krsna, Hare Rama Maha Mantra while preparing and performing the act.

PAST LIVES SERMON

Past Lives must not be thought upon too much, because Past Lives cause distractions from the Path of Truth. The Monks and Nuns of Neo-Aum must advance past such minor things as Past Lives, in order to attain True Enlightenment. Past Lives are the reason we are all here, however that is not always a bad thing, because Sri Vishnu is the Master of the Universe, and it is His will which brought Humanity The Supreme Truth. The Monks and Nuns of Neo-Aum were also brought to Me by the grace of Sri Vishnu, who called out to their Soul to receive these Teachings.

REPETITION SERMON

In order to prevent the Monks and Nuns of Neo-Aum from falling into Error, I deem it to be needed that all Monks and Nuns get into the habit of Repeating one Sermon each Night before Bed, and each Morning upon Waking. I advise keeping a copy of the Sermons by the Bed, and repeating them once in Bed, and before leaving the Bed, this will allow the deeper Message of these Teachings to enter into the mind, to be pondered while Awake and while Asleep. It is also Required that a Monk or Nun recites the Hare Krsna, Hare Rama Maha Mantra Before and After performing Repetition of the Sermons.

SOCIETY SERMON

I have observed Society becoming more and more Spiritually Sick, very few people focus on anything except pointless Materialistic subjects, such as how much Money they have, or how big of a House they have, or etc., the list goes on and on. Neo-Aum is against this Spiritually Sick Society, that deserves nothing less than Total Destruction in Honor of Sri Vishnu, so that a New Spiritual Society shall be built upon the Ashes and Rubble of the Old Society. The New Spiritual Society shall grow its Gardens using the Cremated remains of the Sinful, who chose not to Join Neo-Aum, so they were Murdered by Sri Kalki, as Punishment for their Sinful Acts and Life.

FIRST VISION

World Governments shall turn their weapons upon one another, as a result of distrust at which point War shall occur, leading to the use of weapons of a Biological and, or Chemical nature. Seeing this shall begin causing paranoia among most Countries, which shall bring destabilization to those Countries, at which point Wars within those Places shall break out, and much Sin shall be committed.

SECOND VISION

Mass Murder shall occur as Entire Countries Cannibalize themselves, all crime will no longer be contained. There will be no Police to save anyone, as they shall be attempting to defend themselves, or they will already be dead. The Bodies of Men, Women and Children shall be thrown in the streets, left to rot or be gnawed on by wild animals, insects and rodents. Death by various Plagues shall reduce the number of Children born, as well as reduce the number of people in general upon the Earth. Then the Toxic Mushrooms shall sprout across the Planet as the World Governments destroy each other with Nuclear Weapons.

THIRD VISION

The Last Avatar of Sri Vishnu, known as Sri Kalki shall then present himself, and guide his Monks and Nuns to Exterminate all Unenlightened and Sinful people who are still alive. All Murder, All Cannibalism and All Sexual perversions shall be allowed by Sri Kalki as a reward for all Monks and Nuns who have shown Absolute Loyalty, Faith and Devotion.

GEARS SERMON

People in America believe that individuality is absolutely needed in order to be a "free" person. Such an idea is incorrect because a Society that encourages individuality only does so to enslave the masses and make people incapable of forming together to overthrow the leaders of that society. Unlike the disgusting individualistic Society which is embodied in America, Neo-Aum sees its Monks and Nuns as Gears, which aid in the turning of the Dharma Wheel faster and faster, bringing the appearance of Sri Kalki closer by the day.

HOLY WARRIOR SERMON

The Monks and Nuns of Neo-Aum are Holy Warriors who answer to no Law, but that of the Supreme Authority of Sri Vishnu and Neo-Aum. Monks and Nuns must understand that they are Not to concern themselves with their own Health, but are instead to concern themselves with only the Health of Neo-Aum by advancing the Holy Will of Sri Vishnu. The Monks and Nuns must be willing to leave their Material Bodies if that will aid Neo-Aum in its Sacred Goal, which is to Destroy this Materialistic Society and Create a Spiritual Society.

THE CALLING SERMON

I Call upon all who feel that they could advance the cause of Sri Vishnu by Joining Neo-Aum to contact me and Join. I offer nothing more and nothing less than Absolute Devotion to Sri Vishnu, because Absolute Devotion is everything. As a Monk or Nun of Neo-Aum, I require You to Send Writings and Experiences You have after Joining Neo-Aum to me on my Email or Message Me on My personal Facebook. The Writings shall be compiled and possibly published at a later date. All people involved with Neo-Aum must contribute to the cause of Sri Vishnu by spreading the Message which I have taught through these Sermons.

WAR SERMON

I must advise You, that all Monks and Nuns are only allowed to Participate in War to advance the Holy Cause of Sri Vishnu. They shall not be allowed in a War for Sinful and Materialistic Reasons. The Only Way a Monk or Nun shall be able to get Approval from Neo-Aum to Partake in War, is if that War is only in Honor of Sri Vishnu.

RACE SERMON

I have never been Racist, because Racism binds Your Mind to Materialistic things such as Skin Color or Nationality, which takes Your focus away from Sri Vishnu. I believe all people should be treated in the way that they are most useful, regardless of Race, but all people who just desire Material things their entire life, deserve to be at the bottom of a pile of Corpses, destined only for Cremation.

BLACK ROOM SERMON

I have found that Meditation is most effective in Total Darkness, which is the reason that I require all Monks and Nuns who are part of Neo-Aum to acquire a space within their place of dwelling which they must either paint black, or keep completely Dark during Meditation. The Black Room should be used each night as a way to get closer to Sri Vishnu, who is the Source of all things of both a Material and Spiritual Nature.

DEVINE SERVICE SERMON

I have came to the conclusion through Meditation upon Sri Vishnu that all things which are called "Evil" by the Non-Devotees in this Materialistic and Sinful World which We currently Exist In, should be used by Devotees to Honor Sri Vishnu. No matter how Grotesque these Acts are, as long as You do these Acts for Sri Vishnu, they shall be Called Devine Service.

SLEEP SERMON

An Advanced Devotee of Sri Vishnu can function on only a few Hours of Sleep. I require all Monks and Nuns of Neo-Aum to Force Themselves to stay awake past their usual Sleep Schedule, which will aid the Advancement of all Devotees upon The Path of Truth. The reason for this is because Sleep is not of great importance to Neo-Aum, because Sleep takes the focus of the Monks and Nuns away from Sri Vishnu.

ALMS SERMON

All Monks and Nuns Must Pay Alms and Donate all Materialistic Possessions to Neo-Aum. Paying Alms is required in order to Advance the Goal of Creating a New Spiritual Society, where all Property shall be Owned only by Sri Vishnu and Neo-Aum, which will prevent Sinful behaviors, and will keep The New Society focused only upon Spirituality and Fanatical Devotion to Sri Vishnu.

OVERPOPULATION SERMON

Overpopulation is a Major Problem which must be Addressed. The Human Population continues to Grow due to so many Humans being allowed to simply Breed as they choose without any Control over them by an outside Force. In the New Spiritual Society All Breeding will be Sanctioned only by Sri Kalki, and carefully Documented and Controlled by Neo-Aum. In the New Society, all People Who Fail to Receive Approval from Sri Kalki, and get their Breeding Documented by Neo-Aum, shall be Punished Harshly and then Cleansed from the Earth under the Supreme Authority and Supreme Wisdom of Sri Kalki.

UTOPIA SERMON

I created Neo-Aum out of an act of Pure Devotion to Sri Vishnu, to pave the Glorious way for Sri Kalki, the Final Avatar of Sri Vishnu, whose mission is to Cleanse this World of all Sinful and Unenlightened Humans with the Aid of Neo-Aum. Once all Sinful and Unenlightened Humans are removed from Earth, Neo-Aum shall be Trusted to build a Utopia upon the Bones of the Billions who Sri Kalki shall Cleanse from the Earth. The Utopia will be a perfect Society, in which Sri Kalki shall rule with Ultra-Totalitarian and Ultra-Authoritarian Power. In this Utopia, the Daily Practices of All Monks and Nuns shall be Monitored by Neo-Aum under the direct Guidance of our Holy Dictator Sri Kalki. The Utopia will be of a Totally Spiritual nature, in which the Supreme Truth is Taught to all from Birth to Death. Any Monk or Nun that questions the Authority of Sri Kalki, shall be Immediately Punished by Neo-Aum , then they will be Cleansed from the Earth, for in the Utopia which We aim to create, all Sinful Acts will be Punished without Mercy, no matter How Young or How Old the Sinner is. If the Description of this Utopia Scares You, then You are one of the Sinful and Unenlightened Humans who Sri Kalki shall Cleanse from the Earth. If the Description of this Utopia brings Excitement and Joy to Your Soul, then You should Join Neo-Aum, and become a Soldier of Sri Kalki, for it is People like You Who shall Flourish in Neo-Aum and shall aid in building the Holy Utopia.

DEMOCRACY SERMON

I must Warn all Who are Reading this, if Your Country is a Democracy, then it shall Collapse if it Stays under that Political System, at which point the Governments shall Turn upon their People, and Civil War and Chaos shall begin. Totalitarianism is the Future Political System of the entire Planet, for Sri Kalki shall take Total Control of This World and Every Person in it. I have this to say to All People Who are Reading this Sermon, You have Two choices. Choice One is that You may Choose to attempt to Defend and Hold up Democracy when it begins to Crumble. This shall result in You being Crushed and Killed when it fully Falls on You, leaving only the Broken and Bloody Organic Vehicle which You once called a Body under the many others Who tried to prevent the fall of Democracy. Choice Two is that You aid in the Fall of Democracy, so that it can be Replaced with an Ultra-Totalitarian Utopia which shall be under the Holy Dictatorship of Sri Kalki. If You want the System of Democracy to continue to Exist, then You shall be placed upon Piles of Corpses and Cleansed from the Earth by Sri

Kalki, but If You Desire the Total Fall of Democracy, so that a New Utopian Society can be built, then Join Neo-Aum, For You shall be of Great Importance to the Glorious plan of Sri Kalki.

MOST DEVOTED SERMON

I am looking for only the Most Devoted, which are People Who wish to Join Neo-Aum, and become Monks and Nuns Who are Willing to Fight and even Leave Their Organic Vehicles out of Fanatical Devotion and Faith in Sri Vishnu. I am Looking for People Who understand that this World We currently Live In is Infested with Sinful and Spiritually Sick Humans that must be Cleansed from this World so that a New World can be built upon the Remains of the Old Sinful World and The Ashes of the Sinful and Materialistic People shall be used to Grow Crops and Aid in Agricultural Production in the New Society.

CANNIBAL SERMON

Cannibalism can Aid in Reducing the Problem of Overpopulation, and at the same time can help Reduce the Issue of Mass Starvation in many Countries. The Monks and Nuns of Neo-Aum understand that When the Sinful and

Materialistic Countries begin to Cannibalize Themselves, as foretold in The Second Vision, it is indeed likely that Humanity will be Cannibalizing Each Other as well. I approve of Cannibalism because Humanity must be Reduced, and When Sri Kalki Arrives, it is very likely that Eating the Flesh of Men, Women and Children will be a Normal Practice in The New and Beautiful World which is to Come.

THE REVOLUTION SERMON

Neo-Aum is a Revolutionary Movement which seeks to Totally Destroy the Current World, so that a New Spiritual World can be Built in its Place by all Who are Enlightened by The Supreme Truth. All Who Fight against Neo-Aum, Shall be Punished, and Cleansed from the Earth by Sri Vishnu in His Final Form as Sri Kalki and All Must be Warned that Sri Kalki Will not Spare those Who Resist Enlightenment and Truth. Neo-Aum Seeks to Prepare this World for The Arrival of Sri Kalki, All Who wish to Stay in Their Organic Vehicles Through the Arrival of Sri Kalki, Must Join Neo-Aum. Those Who are Unenlightened will not Believe the Truth Which I am Writing, and for Their Ignorance They will be Punished and Their Organic Vehicles shall be Destroyed.

BLOOD SERMON

Blood must be Spilled as an Offering to Sri Vishnu in Order for the Arrival of Sri Kalki to Occur, from which a Sea of Blood shall Cover the Earth. The Sea of Blood shall be the Blood of the Unenlightened Masses which cling only to Materialism and Sinful Action to Sustain Themselves. The Unenlightened Masses Shall be Cut Down by Sri Kalki, for They are Sinners and must not be allowed to Exist in Their Organic Vehicles. Once Sri Kalki Cuts down the Unenlightened Masses of Humanity, the World Shall be Covered in Blood, but this Blood shall not Stay. The Blood shall Soak into the Earth and From it Agriculture shall Flourish and the New Society shall Exist For All Time Under the Devine Guidance of Sri Kalki.

BAD KARMA SERMON

Bad Karma can only be Removed through Fanatical Devotion to Sri Vishnu and by Punishing all Members of Neo-Aum who bring Bad Karma. These Punishments shall Remove the Bad Karma From The Monk or Nun, so that The Rest of Neo-Aum stays Spiritually Clean in the Eyes of Sri Vishnu. Punishments can be Minor or Severe, Depending upon How Sinful the Monk or Nun Was which Caused the Bad Karma. Once Punishment is Authorized, it Must be Carried out by Neo-Aum Upon the Sinner, regardless of the Circumstances of The Sin, or the Age of the Sinner.

ENEMIES OF NEO-AUM SERMON

All Monks and Nuns of Neo-Aum Must Hold Complete and Fanatical Hatred for all Unenlightened People. Hate Them, for this is The Holy Will Sri Vishnu, for They are The Enemies of Neo-Aum. All Enemies Must be Punished Without Mercy, and Cleansed Without Sympathy from All Places upon Earth. Sri Kalki Will Slaughter The Enemies without Mercy, He Will Perform a Holy Mass Cleansing of The Earth. We Must act as Sri Kalki, and Do as He Does, For He is Who We Serve.

DEVINE ORDERS SERMON

When Neo-Aum Gives You an Order, You Must Follow that Order, for it is of a Devine Nature. All Monks and Nuns of Neo-Aum are Expected to Obey all Orders Spoken to Them by Neo-Aum, Those Who do Not Obey shall be Punished without Mercy or Understanding. Disobedience will Not be Tolerated by Neo-Aum, for if a Monk or Nun is Not Willing to Obey the Devine Will of Neo-Aum, They shall be Cleansed from the Earth when Sri Kalki

Arrives, for They are Sinful and Tainted with Unenlightenment. Sri Kalki shall Issue Orders When He Arrives upon Earth, and all of His Orders Must be Followed with Fanatical Devotion, No matter How "Horrific" or "Evil" His Orders might sound to the Unenlightened Masses of Human Filth which Exist Upon the Earth at this Current Day in this Stage of The Kali Yuga.

MONEY SERMON

I Find it Sad How The Unenlightened Masses Waste Their Entire Lives Trying to get Money so that They Can feed Their Sinful and Materialistic Ways. I Admit that Neo-Aum has to Have some Money to Develop and Grow, but that Money is only a Means to an End. Neo-Aum shall remove the Need for Money in the New Spiritual Society which Sri Kalki shall Create. Money is Materialistic and Sinful because it Inspires People to be Materialistic and Sinful, and that is Precisely Why all Money must be Destroyed. Once Money is Destroyed and All Sinful and Materialistic People are Cleansed from The Earth by Sri Kalki. All Humans shall only then Discover the Supreme Truth and Live a Totally Spiritual Life through the Glory of Sri Vishnu.

COW SERMON

In the New Spiritual Society, the Slaughter of Cows shall be Forbidden. Cows will be for Producing Milk and New Cows for those Many Monks and Nuns Within the Holy Utopia. the Only time Cow Slaughter could Occur is Under the Direct Authority of Sri Kalki, and anyone Who is Caught Slaughtering Cows without Permission From Sri Kalki, shall be Cleansed from the Earth Immediately, for Cow Slaughter is not just an Unforgivable Sin against the other Monks and Nuns, but Cow Slaughter is Also an Unforgivable Sin Against Sri Kalki Himself.

M.P.O.B. SERMON

Neo-Aum understands that Blood has many useful Magical Properties, which can Benefit The Monks and Nuns Who are willing to Drink Cleansed Blood. The Meaning of Cleansed is that the Blood has been Purified by Reciting the Hare Krsna, Hare Rama Maha Mantra. The Recitation of the Maha Mantra Opens The Blood to Blessings by the Holy Power of Sri Vishnu. Once the Blood is Cleansed, the Monk or Nun Must then Drink The Cleansed Blood, which will allow Each Monk or Nun to Attain the M.P.O.B. (Magical Properties of Blood).

RITUAL WASHING SERMON

All Monks and Nuns of Neo-Aum Must Perform Ritual Washing Once Before Sleeping, and Once Upon Waking. Ritual Washing Should be performed by Taking a Shower or Bath while Focusing Deeply Upon Sri Vishnu, and Chanting the Hare Krsna, Hare Rama Maha Mantra. The Ritual Washing is only Complete when Every Part of The Organic Vehicle has been Cleansed by the Water. Ritual Washing Must be Performed Daily, but if a Monk or Nun does Not Perform Ritual Washing Each Day then Bad Karma shall Infest the Monk or Nun, and Sri Vishnu shall become Angry.

EARTH SERMON

Earth is being Destroyed by the Unenlightened and Materialistic Human Filth which Crawls around this Planet, Eating up Land which should be used for Agricultural Purposes, but Instead The Unenlightened Humans are using the Land for Building Apartments, Stores and Materialistic Things which will bring No Enlightenment into Their Sinful Lives. If We would Cut Down The Unenlightened Humans, at the Same Rate that The Unenlightened Humans Cut down Trees and Rain Forests, The Earth would be Healthy and Clean.

NEO-AUM TEA SERMON

Neo-Aum holds a Sacred Recipe to Brew a Special Tea which shall aid in Enlightenment. Neo-Aum Tea shall Clear the Mind and Cleanse the Soul of Sinful Thoughts and Bad Karma. The Tea is Brewed by Taking Dry Tea Leaves and placing them in a Pot Filled with Water which is over a Flame to Boil the Tea. When the Tea Starts Boiling, The Monk or Nun must Chant the Hare Krsna, Hare Rama Maha Mantra. This shall Prepare the Tea, and Aid in its Enlightening Effects upon the Monk or Nun. Sake Should be Added before Drinking the Tea, this is an approved Alcohol which Monks and Nuns may Drink if mixed with Neo-Aum Tea. After A Monk or Nun Consumes Neo-Aum Tea, The Monk or Nun Must then Sit and Meditate while chanting the Hare Krsna, Hare Rama Maha Mantra while Focusing on The Three Visions.

INDIVIDUAL MIND, ORGANIC VEHICLE AND SOUL SERMON

The Individual Mind and Organic Vehicle are Separate from The Soul, this is due to the Fact that the Soul is Ageless and Originates Directly from Sri Vishnu, while The Individual Mind and The Organic Vehicle are from Sri Vishnu, as are All Other Things, They are Materialistic and Must be Removed so that Only The Soul

Remains. The Organic Vehicle and The Individual Mind are both The Cause of All Illusions Which Lead to the Accumulation of Bad Karma. The Mind and The Organic Vehicle Must be Changed Spiritually and Physically through Deep Meditation, Spiritual Practice and Fanatical Devotion to Sri Vishnu.

NEO-AUM SERMONS

www.ingramcontent.com/pod-product-compliance
Lightning Source LLC
Chambersburg PA
CBHW071752020426
42331CB00008B/2292